Much Ado About Nothing SASKIA REEVES

Saskia Reeves was born in London and trained at the Guildhall School of Music and Drama. She has played a number of Shakespearean roles including Hermia, Isabella, Regan and Beatrice. Her stage tions for Cheek By Jowl, Theatre, the Royal Cou Warehouse and she has Nicholas Hytner, Declan Steven Berkoff and Katie Mi

She has premiered in a range of contemporary plays – by Caryl Churchill, Stephen Poliakoff, Tom Kempinski – in addition to work by Edward Albee and Tennessee Williams.

As well as a varied television career, Saskia has starred in some of the most challenging British films of the decade since her feature debut in *December Bride* (Thaddeus O'Sullivan), these include *Close My Eyes* (Stephen Poliakoff), *Butterfly Kiss* (Michael Winterbottom), *Heart* (Charles McDougall) and most recently *The Tesseract* (Oxide Pang).

Colin Nicholson is the originator and editor for the Actors on Shakespeare series published by Faber and Faber.

in the same series

SASKIA REEVES

Much Ado About Nothing

Series Editor: Colin Nicholson

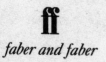

faber and faber

First published in 2003
by Faber and Faber Limited
3 Queen Square London WC1N 3AU

Typeset by Faber and Faber in Minion
Printed in England by Mackays of Chatham, plc

A CIP record for this book
is available from the British Library

ISBN 0–571–21633–1

10 9 8 7 6 5 4 3 2 1

Introduction

Shakespeare: Playwright, Actor and Actors' Playwright

It is important to remember that William Shakespeare was an actor, and his understanding of the demands and rewards of acting helped him as a playwright to create roles of such richness and depth that actors in succeeding generations – even those with no reason or desire to call themselves 'classical' actors – have sought opportunities to perform them.

As the company dramatist, Shakespeare was writing under the pressure of producing scripts for almost immediate performance by his fellow players – the Lord Chamberlain's Men (later the King's Men), who, as a share-holding group, had a vested interest in their playhouse. Shakespeare was writing for a familiar set of actors: creating roles for particular players to interpret; and, being involved in a commercial enterprise, he was sensitive to the direct contact between player and audience and its power to bring in paying customers. His answer to the challenge produced a theatrical transformation: Shakespeare peopled the stage with highly credible personalities, men and women who were capable of change, and recognizable as participants in the human condition which their audience also shared. He connected two new and important elements: the idea of genuine individuality – the solitary, reflecting, self-communing soul, which is acutely aware of its own sufferings and desires; and, correlatively, the idea of inner life as something that not only exists but can also be explored. For him, the connection became the motor of dramatic action on the stage, as it is the motor of personal action in real life.

The primary importance of the actor cannot be disputed: it is his or her obligation – assisted to a greater or lesser extent by a director's overall vision of the play – to understand the personality they are representing onstage and the nature of the frictions taking place when that personality interacts with other characters in the drama: Shakespeare's achievement goes far beyond the creation of memorable characters (Macbeth, Falstaff) to embrace the exposition of great relationships (Macbeth–Lady Macbeth; Falstaff–Prince Hal). Great roles require great actors, and there is no group of people in a better position to interpret those roles to *us* than the principal actors of *our* generation – inhabitants of a bloodline whose vigour resonates from the sixteenth century to the present day – who have immersed themselves in the details of Shakespeare's creations and have been party to their development through rehearsal and performance.

Watching Shakespeare can be an intimidating experience, especially for those who are not well versed in the text, or in the conventions of the Elizabethan stage. Many excellent books have been written for the academic market but our aim in this series is somewhat different. *Actors on Shakespeare* asks contemporary performers to choose a play of particular interest to them, push back any formal boundaries that may obstruct channels of free communication and give the modern audience a fresh, personal view. Naturally the focus for each performer is different – and these diverse volumes are anything but uniform in their approach to the task – but their common intention is, primarily, to look again at plays that some audiences may know well and others not at all, as well as providing an insight into the making of a performance.

Each volume works in its own right, without assuming an in-depth knowledge of the play, and uses substantial quotation to contextualize the principal points. The fresh approach of the many and varied writers will, we hope, enhance your enjoyment of Shakespeare's work.

Colin Nicholson
February 2002

Note: For reference, the text used here is the Arden Shakespeare.

Characters

Don Pedro, *Prince of Aragon*
Don John, *his bastard brother*
Claudio, *a young lord of Florence*
Benedick, *a young lord of Padua*
Leonato, *Governor of Messina*
Antonio, *his brother*
Balthasar, *a singer, attendant on Don Pedro*
Conrade and Borachio, *followers of Don John*
Friar Francis
Dogberry, *master constable*
Verges, *a headborough*
First watchman
Second watchman
A sexton
A boy
A lord
Hero, *daughter to Leonato*
Beatrice, *niece to Leonato*
Margaret and Ursula, *gentlewomen attending on Hero*
Messengers, Musicians, Watchmen, Attendants, etc.

Much Ado About Nothing was presented and toured nationally and internationally by Cheek by Jowl Theatre Company starting on 12 February 1998 at the Everyman Theatre, Cheltenham. The cast was as follows:

THE ARMY

Don Pedro	Stephen Mangan
Don John	Paul Goodwin
Claudio	Bohdan Poraj
Benedick	Matthew Macfadyen
Balthasar	Andrew Price
Borachio	Justin Salinger
Conrade	Mark Lacey
Messenger	Riz Abbasi

LEONATO'S HOUSEHOLD

Leonato	Raad Rawi
Ursula (Antonio)	Ann Firbank
Hero	Sarita Choudhury
Beatrice	Saskia Reeves
Margaret	Zoe Aldrich
Friar Francis	Andrew Price

THE WATCH

Dogberry	Derek Hutchinson
Verges	Sam Beazley
First Watchman	Andrew Price
Second Watchman	Riz Abbasi

Dedicated to Clint and Merlin
and Clapham Public Library

Foreword

The beginning

I played Beatrice in Cheek By Jowl's production of *Much Ado About Nothing*. It was the second time I had worked for them, and the production toured England, went abroad and then settled in the West End for a limited run in the summer of 1998.

Cheek By Jowl Theatre Company is run by Declan Donnellan (the director) and Nick Ormerod (the designer), and *Much Ado About Nothing* was to be their last production for some time. After seventeen years and twenty-five productions, Nick and Declan were ending the company's policy of producing and touring work every year and taking a long break to work abroad. They had created the most wonderful productions of Shakespeare's plays that I had seen, though they did not limit themselves to just Shakespeare. Cheek By Jowl started in 1981 with William Wycherley's Restoration comedy *The Country Wife*, had a huge success with *Vanity Fair* and went on to further acclaim with *A Midsummer Night's Dream* and *As You Like It*. They resurfaced at the Young Vic in 2002 with Tony Kushner's *Homebody/Kabul*, first produced in New York.

If I am being honest, I hadn't really understood Shakespeare or got much pleasure from his plays until I first worked with Cheek By Jowl. I hadn't been acting professionally for very long when I was cast as Hermia in their production of *A Midsummer Night's Dream*. It was the first time I had been asked to improvise in the rehearsal room and it was a revelation to me to be able to do that with Shakespeare. I'd grown to love improvisation as a teenager, going to weekend drama workshops in New Malden, where all we did was improvise. A lot of our end-of-term shows were constructed out of these improvisations and I associated acting with having fun. I hadn't had much fun acting since leaving drama school and I was beginning to think I'd have to give it up or lower my expectations.

Declan's approach to *A Midsummer Night's Dream* was fresh and easily understood, contemporary and very, very funny. I saw another way of approaching Shakespeare. I'd always felt nervous of him: I thought you needed a degree to understand him and I hadn't even passed my A levels. I now know that his writing is more robust. His language can be powerful as well as beautiful, and rough as well as eloquent. Shakespeare was writing for a diverse audience, the uneducated and poor as much as the rich and cultured. It's a shame that it isn't usually as mixed in a theatre nowadays. Cheek By Jowl always toured extensively, which gave me the chance to play Shakespeare to all sorts of audiences (from the Muslim children in Pashawar to the wealthy Italians in Sicily). It had been a breakthrough of sorts, working on that play, and the experience had turned me around.

Declan asked me to audition for Beatrice. In those intervening thirteen years I had performed another four of Shakespeare's plays, each with a different company, but my appreciation hadn't really developed since *A Midsummer Night's Dream*. I was very excited by the prospect of working with the company again, but surprised by the role, as I had never considered myself as a 'Beatrice'. Hermia had felt more right – 'though she be but little, she is fierce' – so had Viola in *Twelfth Night*, Isabella in *Measure For Measure*, Regan in *King Lear* and Silvia in *The Two Gentlemen Of Verona*. I realized, from my hesitation, that I probably had a more conventional approach than I cared to admit. I wasn't helped by the attitude of a drama teacher who had told me I would never play Cleopatra. I don't know what it was that she felt I fell so short of in this role (she thought Googie Withers a perfect Cleopatra), but I was easily intimidated. If I would never play Cleopatra, it simply followed in my mind that I would never play Beatrice either. To me, convention dictated that Beatrice was tall (I had seen Janet McTeer play her, directed by Matthew Warchus), a spinster (Elizabeth Spriggs played her middle-aged) and not just funny but hilarious (Maggie Smith played Beatrice to Robert Stephens's Benedick).

'We are all mortal'

The Royal Shakespeare Company illustrates its programmes with photographs of previous productions and I was scaring myself with my own imagined programme for *Much Ado About Nothing* with all the previous great and good Beatrice and Benedicks: Judi Dench–Donald Sinden, Peggy Ashcroft–John Gielgud . . . I couldn't yet visualize Saskia Reeves and Matthew Macfadyen (no offence, Matthew!). I think this is true with any actor about to take on one of Shakespeare's roles and considering the hundreds of people that have played the part before, some famously so – just think if you had to play Hamlet! With Beatrice you can add to the list Ellen Terry, Katharine Hepburn, Sybil Thorndike, Felicity Kendal and Emma Thompson. However, I trusted Declan and I was very happy to audition, even if I was scared.

Declan asked me to read opposite Matthew Macfadyen, who already had the part of Benedick. This made me more nervous. What if the audition went well but we didn't fit together somehow? What if Matthew didn't like me? What if I didn't like Matthew? And I realized I hardly knew the play at all. I did not yet understand any of the levels within the story. Reading the play, or even seeing it in performance, does not give you the information you need to act it out.

I had to prepare the first dialogue between Beatrice and Benedick in Act I, scene i. I learned this small exchange without really knowing what it was, or who I was pretending to be, even though I'd read the play from beginning to end by then. Together we read the scene a few times and, little by little, I began to fall for this character Beatrice. She had lines like: 'I wonder that you will still be talking, Signior Benedick: nobody marks you,' and, 'I had rather hear my dog bark at a crow than a man swear he loves me.' I was pleasantly surprised that we were all at a point of discovery with these characters. Matthew didn't seem to be as far ahead as I had feared – or at least he didn't make me feel as if he was – and Declan, too, admitted to not knowing what it was all about yet. The scene was undoubtedly funny; but because I had no idea who these people were, I could only admire the writing and the wonderful structure of the dialogue. It was witty and you could sense a balance between their intellects and temperaments. A good quote from our programme was: 'Wit is a sword. It is meant to make people feel the point as well as see it' (G. K. Chesterton); but what these characters were actually trying to do and whether they were successful and what was going on underneath, I didn't know.

When I accepted the offer of the part and started working on it properly, I remembered all the things that had made working with Cheek By Jowl such a good experience. *Much Ado About Nothing* was so different in style and content from *A Midsummer Night's Dream*, but the ways in which we worked to discover the play and the characters were similar. We would do all sorts of things as well as rehearse the scenes in a traditional sense. We improvised around the story to give our characters shared experiences and background information. There were explorations of themes in the play, a lot of movement and text work, and songs and dances to be learnt. Everyone would be singing, and if we could play a musical instrument, we were encouraged to do so. The rehearsal time was longer than for *A Midsummer Night's Dream*, additionally involving a musical director, Paddy Cuneen, and a movement director, Jane Gibson, who spent as much time rehearsing with us as possible. Declan continued to rehearse the play throughout the run. This was something I really enjoyed about working with Cheek By Jowl: I was able to keep discovering the character as I went along and I had the chance to improve.

Performing would be a whole different experience from rehearsing. I know I got better in the part from when I started in Cheltenham to when I finished at the Playhouse Theatre in London. I had performed in so many contrasting theatres, the largest being the Brooklyn Academy of Music in New York. This is a beautiful theatre that Peter Brook helped to design, but it is huge, with over a thousand seats. We had to make changes in the staging here, and we had to project even further. I had no choice but to be bigger in the part and this helped me enormously – I think I literally grew as Beatrice: she became bigger in stature, voice and personality, which was very useful!

Nick never imposed a design for the production at the beginning. This meant he had to be in rehearsals nearly as often as the director and then be prepared to design very quickly. The set had to be flexible enough to fit all the variously sized theatres, and this lent a unique element to his designs that gave Cheek By Jowl part of its style. I found it refreshing not to have to look at a miniature set on the first day of rehearsal, or a drawing of what my character would wear. It was certainly a more inspirational way of working, to be allowed a certain degree of freedom at the beginning. Ideas would change, of course, and some continued to change after we opened, which could be frustrating and demanded patience; but it felt healthier this way and kept us alert even after a four-month run, though I certainly didn't find it easy.

'Sigh no more, ladies'

In the absence of a prepared design there were no pre-production meetings as such. However, an important decision had been made: to change Leonato's brother Antonio into a woman. Ursula the maid would become Ursula the aunt (played by Anne Firbank). Along the same lines, the part of the Sexton would be played by a woman – Zoe Aldridge – and the lines were changed or cut accordingly: 'brother' became 'sister', and so on. Declan had previously directed an all-male cast in *As You Like It* and made two of the mechanicals women in *A Midsummer Night's Dream*. These were decisions that were difficult to change during rehearsals. In *Much Ado About Nothing* there was a lot to be gained by having an Ursula instead of an Antonio. It opened up the question of the women in the play, and I saw Ursula as a possible mirror for Beatrice – what choices does a woman have if she rejects marriage and a family of her own? Was Ursula a possible projection of her future? There was the obvious addition to the group of women in the household, having an aunt instead of an uncle; and rather than an elderly gentleman or patriarch you had a dowager, leaving Leonato as the only man at the head of the family. I couldn't say what was lost, because I didn't know any different. I only know how strong the scenes were, including this older woman; and changing a character's sex helped question any preconceived ideas we might have had about this old and well-known play.

Initially I thought *Much Ado About Nothing* was a happy comedy, little realizing how dark the play was. The story begins with the end of a war, with people wanting to enjoy themselves. The soldiers of the army are amongst women again. One of the soldiers wants to marry. A marriage is arranged to the woman he loves (who also happens to be the richest), and for a laugh, the most unlikely couple are to be manipulated into marrying one another. Deceits and plots are hatched and lies told and believed. An innocent woman's reputation is ruined. A man challenges his best friend to a duel. The truth is uncovered. The woman's honour is restored and in the end two marriages do take place.

It would be simplistic to think you can just do the text. There was a darkness here that could never be brushed aside as something that got in the way of the comedy, because it was part of the spirit of the play. I didn't know this when I started. The same could be said of my understanding of Beatrice. I discovered a mass of contradictions. She jokes constantly, laughing at the expense of others, only to be mortified when she learns that they think her incapable of loving. I had thought Beatrice wouldn't care what others thought of her, but she does – so she couldn't be as secure and self-confident as I had thought she was. So does she mean everything she says?

When you act in a play, you have to approach it with as open a mind as possible. When you can see behind your attitude, you begin to actually see the play, and you discover the blood in the bones of the story. This is especially true of such an old play that carries with it so many expectations. The expectation that all the words of the text should be alive to us today, for instance, is a high expectation. There will always be things we don't know. Declan would say, 'We can't know everything and it doesn't have to be perfect.' I especially liked hearing that last part.

'Men were deceivers ever'

How do you make an old play entertaining to an audience today? How do you act out the themes in the play so that people can relate to them now? Who are these characters?

What sort of setting do you give a play:

Where society is split between the men and the women?

Where a prince can come and stay at your home with his army?

Where marriages are arranged?

Where people wear disguises to a party?

Where marriage is society's main objective for women?

Where a bachelor is acceptable but a spinster is not?

Where a husband is chosen for you?

Where a daughter does what her father tells her?

Where people talk about each other?

Where a woman is valued if she is a virgin, beautiful, rich and doesn't say very much in public (and not necessarily in that order)?

Where a woman retires as a nun if her reputation is ruined?

Where a woman can ask her suitor to kill a man as a matter of honour?

Where a man has the final word?

We needed to find a world that would bring all this together – a relatively modern time, so that the actors and the audience had something to relate to. The Edwardian era gave us the structure we were looking for; the themes didn't seem so old when you put them inside this framework, and in fact they became the more believable for it.

Act I

Wit is the epitaph of an emotion.
Nietzsche (1844–1900)

'I learn in this letter . . .'

Act I took a long time to solve. Shakespeare doesn't give any settings as such, and Messina is somewhere in Sicily; but these characters aren't particularly Italian, only their names seem to be. The men returning from war are variously described as Lords of Aragon, Florence and Padua, but it is difficult to place this army as specifically Italian. (In Shakespeare's day it was the navy that defended England – until Oliver Cromwell's New Model Army in 1645.)

In rehearsals we experimented with a field hospital, trying to bring to life the aspect of war in the story, but it didn't really help much where the women were concerned. I remember trying to get through Beatrice's first lines while pretending to tie bandages and ministering to soldiers lying on imaginary stretchers, but what I was saying wasn't helping what I was doing. I felt clumsy trying to be witty and a nurse at the same time! We needed a social hierarchy: these characters were wealthy, they entertained royalty; so the field hospital was ditched for a more relaxed social occasion in Leonato's country garden.

Leonato, the Governor of Messina, was in our production a wealthy English aristocrat. In scene I he is reading a letter out loud to his household, which a solider has delivered from the Prince, Don Pedro of Aragon. It says the Prince and his army will be arriving that night from the wars and that 'Don Pedro hath bestowed much honour on a young Florentine called Claudio'. This is brilliant news to everyone and the soldier becomes the focus of attention. Beatrice interrupts all this excitement: 'I pray you, is Signior Mountanto returned from the wars or no?' Only Hero knows that she means Benedick, and Beatrice proceeds to insult Benedick, much to the soldier's discomfort. She questions him about Benedick's abilities as a lover – 'Signior Mountanto', a soldier: 'But how many hath he killed? For indeed I promised to eat all of his killing.' She implies he's greedy – 'he is a very valiant trencher-man; he hath an excellent stomach'; stupid – 'In our last conflict four of his five wits went halting off, and now is the whole man governed with one: so that if he have wit enough to keep himself warm, let him bear it for a difference between himself and his horse, for it is all the wealth that he hath left, to be known a reasonable creature'; and fickle – 'he wears his faith but as the fashion of his hat, it ever changes with the next block'; and that he prefers men to women – 'And a good soldier to a lady; but what is he to a lord?'

Benedictus: 'he who is blessed'

We learn a lot about Benedick through Beatrice: he sounds arrogant, cowardly, gluttonous; but, above all, it's the company of men that he really wants. 'I pray you, who is his companion? Is there no young squarer now that will make a voyage with him to the devil?' Beatrice is making everybody laugh at Benedick's expense, and she is enjoying herself enormously; but what she says is strong stuff. To cast doubt on a man's bravery just after he's returned from the wars is not comfortable humour, nor is implying he's homosexual. This is what makes Beatrice so entertaining: she can be witty and shocking at the same time; and she's in there right at the beginning.

She dislikes Benedick. Benedick irritates her; he competes with her and the result is, they fight. 'Hate' is too strong a word, but there is a massive aversion and it feels like an energy inside – almost rage. I can remember feeling like that about someone I was forced to be around – it said a lot about me and where my head was then – but I really disliked this person and I would do everything in my power to avoid them even when we were in the same room. The difference between this scenario and that of Beatrice and Benedick is that I didn't think about this other person all the time. The fact that Benedick, even in his absence, is in the forefront of Beatrice's mind cannot go unnoticed. He's the first thing she talks about: '. . . is Signior Mountanto returned from the wars or no?'; but whatever this signifies – and I deliberately left this unanswered in my imagination – she has turned these feelings into humour. By being funny she hides what she is thinking. But we know she is clever. *She* knows she's clever. Her mind is witty – that's the way her brain works and she has her own particular style. No one can really match her.

On a practical level, she talks about him because he'll be arriving any minute – he's 'not three leagues off' – and his reputation as an entertainer and joker is spoken of by the soldier: 'O, he's returned, and as pleasant as ever he was.' Benedick's her only real competitor, the only person who gives her a good run for her money, but Beatrice has to say she's better than him. He obviously gives her brain the food it needs, though she can't know this because to her he's arrogant and 'no less than a stuffed man; but for the stuffing – well, we are all mortal'.

In Act I, scene i, lines 35–8 are very complicated – 'He set up his bills here in Messina and challenged Cupid at the flight;

and my uncle's fool, reading the challenge, subscribed for Cupid, and challenged him at the bird-bolt' – and in the end we cut them; but we kept the next line about what a braggart she thinks he is and probably a useless soldier more likely to knife a chicken than the enemy: 'I pray you, how many hath he killed and eaten in these wars? But how many hath he killed? For indeed I promised to eat all of his killing.' It wasn't that I didn't understand the beginning of this speech; I found it useful background information, because I always imagined Leonato's fool to be Beatrice herself. To paraphrase, she says: *Benedick posted notices around town to challenge Cupid himself at the sport of love and Leonato's fool stepped in to ridicule Benedick's ambitions as a ladykiller.* I understood the words, but I couldn't get the meaning to land when I spoke them out loud – this was an example of how some of the words will not retain their vitality and wit hundreds of years later. I tried many ways to make the others laugh with this line: I remember improvising this whole section of Act I before the men come on by wearing a red nose, imagining I was a music-hall artist out to entertain; but after having to ask one time too many, 'What was the meaning again . . .?', Declan decided we could cut it. But the line stayed in my memory.

'Don Pedro is approached'

Don Pedro, Prince of Aragon, arrives with all his men. It is all very formal and the women pay their respects to the Prince by curtsying. Leonato introduces his daughter, and then a weird thing happens – well, not so weird, because it highlights the division between the men and the women and what's acceptable in a male-dominated society: the men share a lewd joke, implying Hero's mother slept around:

DON PEDRO . . . I think this is your daughter.

LEONATO Her mother hath many times told me so.

BENEDICK Were you in doubt, sir, that you asked her?
[laughter]

LEONATO Signior Benedick, no, for then were you a child.
[more laughter]

DON PEDRO You have it full, Benedick; we may guess by this
what you are, being a man . . . [big laughter]

And so we meet Benedick and the first thing he does is make
a joke – a dirty joke – that makes all the men laugh. Leonato
takes up the idea, and when the Prince joins in, they're thor-
oughly enjoying themselves.

Beatrice found this all very boring and not very funny, but
of course you wouldn't know it except for a little turn to look
at the audience when Benedick says, 'Were you in doubt, sir,
that you asked her?' This was one of Benedick's defining
features, he laughed at his own jokes – how very irritating;
and Beatrice let the audience know this thought.

I should describe Benedick at this point, because it is
important to realize that all the allusions to him being a
ladies' man were almost feasible in our telling of the story.
Matthew Macfadyen as Benedick was big, broad and dashing,
with a moustache over a stupid grin. Benedick is a warm
character, not a cool, calculating cad, but also an utterly
pompous twit, making silly jokes that only other fools would
find funny; conceited, overbearing and a swaggerer. How
could women possibly find him attractive? God only knows.

'Lady Disdain'

When the Prince and Leonato talk aside and Benedick is left a
little stranded (the only one left to laugh when he says, 'If

Signior Leonato be her father, she would not have his head on her shoulders for all Messina, as like him as she is'), Beatrice cuts him down to size.

Beatrice would make the audience laugh and had them on her side with: 'I wonder that you will still be talking, Signior Benedick: nobody marks you'; Benedick would involve the women in the audience against her: 'But it is certain I am loved of all ladies, only you excepted' – leaving Beatrice out in the cold – 'and I would I could find in my heart that I had not a hard heart, for truly I love none.' She would get the women back on her side with: 'A dear happiness to women, they would else have been troubled with a pernicious suitor. I thank God and my cold blood, I am of your humour for that; I had rather hear my dog bark at a crow than a man swear he loves me.'

Benedick says something very misogynistic, and then Beatrice is just plain rude. They resort to basic insults and Benedick walks off, bringing the whole thing to an abrupt halt. Beatrice feels this is not at all the behaviour of a gentleman, but typical behaviour from Benedick – she'll get her own back on him, though:

BENEDICK God keep your ladyship still in that mind, so some gentleman or other shall scape a predestinate scratched face.

BEATRICE Scratching could not make it worse, and 'twere such a face as yours were.

BENEDICK Well, you are a rare parrot-teacher.

BEATRICE A bird of my tongue is better than a beast of yours.

BENEDICK I would my horse had the speed of your tongue, and so good a continuer. But keep your way, a God's name, I have done.

BEATRICE You always end with a jade's trick, I know you of old.

They manage to pull one another apart, and are often a millimetre away from being humiliated themselves.

There is a lot of humour, in a chauvinistic vein, at the expense of women – 'scratched face', 'parrot-teacher', 'speed of your tongue'; the showy, ostentatious males don't understand the females, the fairer sex, and I would go so far as to say they fear them. Beatrice is witty and outspoken, characteristics that make her undesirable. Women attempting any sort of independence are reduced to a cliché, being labelled 'catty', 'vixen', 'shrew', 'fishwife', 'spinster' by men, their ruling class in this aristocratic society, and kept firmly in their place. Marriage and the home are the women's domain. Beatrice has an incredible mind, and isn't interested in falling in love or getting married. She is bright and can't help being so. How could she compromise her intelligence by being reduced to a subservient housekeeping role? So she stands out by rejecting it; but this isolates her. She sees it happening all around her, most notably in the way her cousin's life is being mapped out for her. Benedick is probably the only man who lets Beatrice be herself but matches her mind word for word. In that respect they are equals; but his chauvinistic view of the world, his authority over her in the world, is what repels her. We see he's no different from any other man, and maybe the least awful only because he's so comical.

She is a feminist, an original, but no pioneer, no politician – just an extremely intelligent woman getting by. I embraced feminism as I grew up and I see in Beatrice how she is afraid she might lose her independence – she might disappear – if she were to marry. I used to be fiercely independent, afraid to commit, because I was actually capable of being too dependent on people or things, and that is a frightening prospect. Then I learned about inter-dependence. Beatrice is not someone to look inwards, but the fear is there, I decided, and if you don't commit, you can't get rejected. The same could be said for Benedick. Fear is what drives these two – the fear of losing their independence, the fear of rejection, and the humiliation that would cause. So it's better to stay where they are. But that is a lonely place, and this society of Messina is not a warm, embracing, supportive one; it is competitive, judgemental, and masculine.

Don Pedro announces to the gathered party that they have been invited to stay as Leonato's guests for 'at the least a month'. There is much audible approval (and a lot of silent disapproval from Beatrice), at which point Don John arrives – the Prince's illegitimate brother. Silence falls, the women curtsy and he is welcomed.

'Marriage sunders friends' – Russian proverb

Benedick and Claudio are left alone, and Claudio admits to him that he would like to marry Hero. Benedick and Claudio are very good friends with strong bonds, as they have fought and won a war together and survived. The Prince has honoured them both, and Claudio wants to know what Benedick thinks about Hero – in all seriousness – cautiously aware that up until now they've stuck together as bachelors and as soldiers, neither one taking the idea of relationships seriously, except the relationship they have enjoyed with each other. It takes a while for Benedick to realize Claudio is serious. Benedick laughs again at his own joke here – 'I noted her not, but I looked on her' – 'noted' is a pun on having sex. *Much Ado About Nothing* was also pronounced 'Much Ado About Noting', meaning 'Much Ado About Sex', which I suppose is what this play is all about. Benedick also calls himself a 'professed tyrant to their [the opposite] sex'. I thought it followed from this that he probably wasn't! Men who always talk about sex are probably the ones who aren't getting it, but I think Benedick has taken on this mantle to entertain his friends and probably he, too, is terrified of women.

Claudio has fallen for Hero and almost immediately idolizes her. The two soldiers' conversation is sexist by today's standards, the world they inhabit is politically incorrect – which made me understand where Beatrice was coming from; but also you see Claudio putting Hero on some kind of pedestal. She's beautiful and rich and he wants her. He objectifies her – but this is an immature and inexperienced suitor speaking who is more used to the company of men.

BENEDICK Would you buy her, that you inquire after her?
CLAUDIO Can the world buy such a jewel?

Don Pedro joins them, wanting to know what they're talking about, and Benedick tells him that Claudio has fallen in love, something Benedick himself will never do: 'I will live a bachelor,' he says. I imagine, too, that if Don Pedro were ever to get married, it would most likely be an arranged marriage to create some political opportunity or other. This is the reality.

Benedick and Beatrice are unconventional; but it's more acceptable for a man to be a bachelor than for a woman to be a spinster. Benedick jokes constantly about hating marriage and the opposite sex – he enjoys himself so much in putting them down – one being synonymous with the other; and the more confident and disparaging he is in his argument, the funnier it is to see what his jokes will lead to.

BENEDICK That a woman conceived me, I thank her: that she brought me up, I likewise give her most humble thanks: but that I will have a recheat winded in my forehead, or hang my bugle in an invisible baldrick, all women shall pardon me. Because I will not do them the wrong to mistrust any, I will do myself the right to trust none: and the fine is, for the which I may go the finer, I will live a bachelor.

DON PEDRO I shall see thee, ere I die, look pale with love.

BENEDICK With anger, with sickness, or with hunger, my lord, not with love: prove that ever I lose more blood with love than I will get again with drinking, pick out mine eyes with a ballad-maker's pen, and hang me up at the door of a brothel-house for the sign of blind Cupid.

DON PEDRO Well, if ever thou dost fall from this faith, thou wilt prove a notable argument.

BENEDICK If I do, hang me in a bottle like a cat and shoot at me, and he that hits me, let him be clapped on the shoulder and called Adam.

When Benedick leaves, Don Pedro and Claudio talk about Hero as a wife for Claudio. Claudio makes sure she has money – 'Hath Leonato any son, my lord?' – and Don Pedro confirms, 'No child but Hero, she's his only heir.' There is no apology here; it is a practical question – that's the way this world works. Don Pedro offers to talk with her father so that Claudio shall have her. The Prince decides that the best way to do this will be at the party Leonato is throwing for them that night.

This is where the play strikes a strange chord – one of those plot lines Shakespeare writes where I always think, 'Why on earth do they do that?' Don Pedro decides to disguise himself as Claudio – it's a masked ball – and pretend to woo Hero on Claudio's behalf, so as to 'take her hearing prisoner with the force / And strong encounter of my amorous tale'. Afterwards he'll tell her father and 'she shall be thine'; and off they go to put the idea into practice.

'I cannot be a man with wishing'

In *Much Ado About Nothing* we wanted to show men familiar with same-sex friendships. In Shakespeare's day homosexuality went on under cover of conventional heterosexual lifestyles, though levels of tolerance and openness to practise have continually varied over the centuries. Homosexuality remained illegal in Britain until the late twentieth century and yet male preserves dominate the Establishment and are vital to our society: the army, the navy, gentlemen's clubs, public schools, Oxbridge, the Church, Parliament – in all of which women are still at a disadvantage.

There was a definite bond between the characters of Claudio and Don Pedro that could clearly be seen in our performance. Don Pedro had 'bestowed much honour on a young Florentine called Claudio'; they were affectionate and physical with each other. Outwardly it was a camaraderie, but in the Prince's case there may have been a hidden agenda. Don Pedro's love may have gone deeper – but his motives were suggested rather than transparent. As Claudio grew further away from him, his loneliness became more apparent. He was an over-close friend, who did the wooing for Claudio and stood by him resolutely to save him from public embarrassment, but then became isolated, as his friend found the woman he wanted to marry, and learned a lesson in humanity. But then, they are from different backgrounds. Don Pedro is of royal blood and therefore by birth has responsibilities that Claudio cannot know about. Don Pedro spoils him and wants him near. Claudio is arrogant and young, very attractive and privileged, basking in the attention of his rich and powerful friend.

I hate being excluded because I am a woman. I know how lucky I am to have been born in England at a time when equal rights and opportunities for women have (mostly) been established, but I felt it keenly when I wasn't allowed to join in with the boys. My granddad was a Freemason, and I still wonder what goes on behind those closed doors. I once made a successful bid, at an auction, for dinner at the Garrick. I wanted to go inside this place, where once no woman was allowed. I resent not being able to go out for an evening on my own, as men do, simply sitting in a bar – alone – having a quiet drink without raising any eyebrows or drawing unwanted attention. I was definitely a tomboy as a child, and most of my playmates were boys; my mother tells me I even tried to pee against trees like my friends could do. I would often come home without my clothes because I would take them off, as she found out, to save them from getting wet. These personal memories and thoughts grew in my mind as I discovered the story we were trying to tell in *Much Ado About Nothing* and the part of Beatrice.

As all the scenes in Act I took place in Leonato's garden, scenes ii and iii naturally became part of this social occasion. The Prince was offered tea and cucumber sandwiches, and polite and relaxed conversations were going on while the more important dialogues emerged, flowing in and out of each other. Ursula [Antonio] comes up to Leonato and tells him she has overheard that the Prince is in love with Hero and that he means to tell her of it that night. So Leonato makes off to tell Hero to prepare herself for an answer (and off Raad Rawi would go, to make a quick change for Act II – we had to leave our quick changes until the last possible moment, or there wouldn't have been anyone left in the garden).

Leonato and Ursula [Antonio] were aristocrats of their time. They followed convention and the manners of the period.

They were snobs, but deep down there was a kindness. Ursula did a lot of the organizing, whether it was of the refreshments or the ball dresses, and the idea that her niece was to be betrothed sooner or later was like a dream come true for her. I think they'd more or less given up on Beatrice; anyway, as a niece she wasn't strictly their problem and she had only herself to blame – no one seemed to want her and she wouldn't listen. Hero, on the other hand, was coming along very nicely: obedient, quiet in public, poised, educated (but not too much) and beautiful.

'Seek not to alter me'

In scene iii we find out what 'a plain-dealing villain' Don John is; he is the darkest character in *Much Ado About Nothing* – Conrade and Borachio are novices by comparison. He is an unhealthily jealous man, cruel and full of hatred, driven by envy and anger, which he focuses on Claudio, his brother's favourite. His description of himself is shocking for its directness:

DON JOHN I had rather be a canker in a hedge than a rose in his [Don Pedro's] grace, and it better fits my blood to be disdained of all than to fashion a carriage to rob love from any: in this, though I cannot be said to be a flattering honest man, it must not be denied but I am a plain-dealing villain. I am trusted with a muzzle and enfranchised with a clog; therefore I have decreed not to sing in my cage. If I had my mouth I would bite; if I had my liberty I would do my liking: in the meantime, let me be that I am, and seek not to alter me.

It is a chilling thing to hear. You find out he will stop at nothing to destroy Claudio. He wants to create a disaster because he knows he can.

Harrow College

21

Harrow Weald Campus, Learning Centre
Brookshill, Harrow Weald, Middx.
HA3 6RR — — 0208 909 6248

Act II

Men seldom make passes
At girls who wear glasses.
    Dorothy Parker (1893–1967)

'Heigh-ho for a husband!'

Beatrice is not interested in getting married, and on the eve
of her cousin's engagement makes sure that her uncle knows
it. She launches into a huge discussion with him on the sub-
ject, pours scorn and derision on the very idea. Hero is getting ready, being dressed for the occasion by her aunt and her
maid, Margaret, almost like a lamb to the slaughter. Beatrice
is on top form; her imagination is alive and sharp, but her
true feelings are buried deep inside. Her cousin, whom she
loves deeply, is about to be betrothed to the Prince. Hero has
no choice, and is probably very nervous. They all are. It's
exciting and nerve-racking, but to Beatrice it is not right. She
makes an attempt to instil some sort of independent thought
into her cousin – 'but yet for all that, cousin, let him be a
handsome fellow, or else make another curtsy and say,
"Father, as it please me"'. However, she also knows she has no
real influence and so the best thing is to entertain her cousin
and make her laugh, because Beatrice feels protective. They
are very different from each other, Beatrice and Hero –
almost opposites. One is the rebel and the other dutiful; one
won't shut up and the other doesn't speak. It would be very
difficult to get a word in at all with someone like Beatrice
around.

In the Edwardian period, at the turn of the twentieth century, to have no father or mother put a young woman at a social disadvantage. I began to have a picture of Beatrice as the niece, who had no inheritance and, although Leonato was her uncle and guardian, no father whom she had to obey (he's never mentioned, so I presumed him dead). This had the advantage of freeing Beatrice from parental control and allowing her more of a voice, much to the disapproval of Aunt Ursula [Uncle Antonio]. I noticed the difference in Leonato saying to Beatrice at the beginning, in scene i, 'Well, niece, I hope to see you one day fitted with a husband,' and to Hero, 'Daughter, remember what I told you: if the Prince do solicit you in that kind, you know your answer.'

We can see Beatrice trying to interfere. The way she talks is the way her mind works; she has a very individual imagination. She takes an idea and tells a story with it and the images are bizarre and different. She changes her mind and her argument to suit herself, and contradicts herself too; her thoughts overlap each other and change meaning mid-sentence. She can take something someone says and flip it over, and then go off into realms of fantasy. She talks about the perfect man, then says she doesn't want one, and anyway not with a beard; then she describes a conversation with the devil, and imagines herself with the bachelors:

BEATRICE Just, if he send me no husband, for the which blessing I am at him upon my knees every morning and evening. Lord, I could not endure a husband with a beard on his face! I had rather lie in the woollen.

LEONATO You may light on a husband that hath no beard.

BEATRICE What should I do with him? Dress him in my apparel and make him my waiting-gentlewoman? He that hath a beard is more than a youth, and he that hath no beard is less than a man; and he that is more than a youth is not for me; and he that is less than a man I am not for him . . .

LEONATO Well then, go you into hell?

BEATRICE No, but to the gate, and there will the Devil meet me like an old cuckold with horns on his head, and say, 'Get you to heaven, Beatrice, get you to heaven, here's no place for you maids.' So deliver I up my apes, and away to Saint Peter, for the heavens; he shows me where the bachelors sit, and there live we as merry as the day is long.

ANTONIO [URSULA] [*To Hero.*] Well, niece, I trust you will be ruled by your father.

BEATRICE Yes, faith, it is my cousin's duty to make curtsy and say, 'Father, as it please you': but yet for all that, cousin, let him be a handsome fellow, or else make another curtsy and say, 'Father, as it please me'.

LEONATO Well, niece, I hope to see you one day fitted with a husband.

BEATRICE Not till God make men of some other metal than earth. Would it not grieve a woman to be over-mastered with a piece of valiant dust, to make an account of her life to a clod of wayward marl? No, uncle, I'll none: Adam's sons are my brethren, and truly I hold it a sin to match in my kindred.

She won't be married to 'a piece of valiant dust', and this is where I think Beatrice shows her fear. Men are flesh and blood, and not perfect. There's no such thing as a perfect man, so she won't have one; but you have to be able to live with the imperfections or you'll always be unhappy. It's all right that it's not perfect – a lesson from the director about acting the play but it also became an insight into my character. No one's perfect – not even Beatrice!

So, deep inside, under all this confidence and humour, I imagined a great deal of insecurity. I remembered when I was a teenager coming into puberty how awkward and ugly I felt. My sister, only a few years younger, was by far the more attractive, I believed. She had freckles where I had spots. She had boys interested in her and I didn't. But because I was older, I refused to let it show that it bothered me, or that I was jealous, because I loved my sister and I knew she wasn't trying to compete. I was the competitive one. So I would end up at these rather sad parties where it would be just me, my sister and a girlfriend of hers, and usually three or four boys, and while my sister and her friend were happily being chatted up or snogged, I was having a horrible time with some boy who had no interest in me, and I made it worse by taking the piss out of him. I would make her leave early because I'd get so bored (secretly jealous and miserable). It took until I was quite a bit older to believe that I was attractive to the opposite sex and give them a break!

Beatrice is constantly being told she won't get a husband:

LEONATO By my troth, niece, thou wilt never get thee a husband, if thou be so shrewd of thy tongue.

ANTONIO [URSULA] In faith, she's too curst.

Earlier, in Act I, scene i, Benedick says of her, '. . . there's her cousin, and she were not possessed with a fury, exceeds her as much in beauty as the first of May doth the last of December.'

Leonato's opinion, expressed in the same scene, is: 'You will never run mad, niece'; and then later, at the party:

DON PEDRO She cannot endure to hear tell of a husband.

LEONATO O, by no means, she mocks all her suitors out of suit.

(Act II, scene i)

Beatrice, making fun of herself says, 'Thus goes everyone to the world but I, and I am sunburnt. I may sit in a corner and cry "Heigh-ho for a husband!"'

These messages that she is not fit to be someone's wife must hurt; but how confusing and complicated, because she looks around and doesn't see marriage as anything particularly desirable.

'The revellers are entering, brother'

The festivities begin. The men enter in their disguises (Benedick was wearing an ass's head) and no one seems to know who they're talking to or dancing with. Don Pedro dances with Hero, Balthasar with Margaret, Ursula with Leonato and finally Beatrice with Benedick. They again insult each other, each speaking as if of a third party, Benedick attempting to get at Beatrice first; but in retaliation she really goes for him this time, fuelled by their previous encounter.

BEATRICE Why, he is the Prince's jester, a very dull fool; only his gift is in devising impossible slanders. None but libertines delight in him, and the commendation is not in his wit, but in his villainy; for he both pleases men and angers them, and then they laugh at him and beat him. I am sure he is in the fleet; I would he had boarded me.

BENEDICK When I know the gentleman, I'll tell him what you say.

BEATRICE Do, do, he'll but break a comparison or two on me, which peradventure not marked, or not laughed at, strikes him into melancholy, and then there's a partridge wing saved, for the fool will eat no supper that night.

They are out to win and hurt and entertain others while doing so. I genuinely believed Beatrice didn't know it was

Benedick she was talking to – that was the way I played it: the audience could make up their own mind. It made it all the worse for Benedick, to think that she would run him down like that behind his back.

Meanwhile, Don John and Borachio track down Claudio:

DON JOHN Are you not Signior Benedick?
CLAUDIO [playing the game] You know me well, I am he.

Then they plant the seed of betrayal and mistrust. They convince Claudio that Don Pedro wishes to marry Hero himself, sending Claudio into a miserable fury, and he goes off to sulk.

'She speaks poniards, and every word stabs'

Don Pedro tells Benedick that he has overstepped the mark with Beatrice this time. Benedick insists it wasn't him who started it, and goes on and on about how awful she is. They have both obviously hit a spot without realizing it. Benedick takes an idea and expands it, exaggerates it, makes it huge; and the bigger it gets, the funnier it gets. The images come tumbling out; he can't stop himself talking; it's almost as if he conjures her up out of his words. I love these lines and the fact that he says he wouldn't marry her . . . well, who said anything about marriage?

An oak but with one green leaf on it would have answered her: my very visor began to assume life and scold with her. She told me, not thinking I had been myself, that I was the Prince's jester, that I was duller than a great thaw, huddling jest upon jest with such impossible conveyance upon me that I stood like a man at a mark, with a whole army shooting at me. She speaks poniards, and every word stabs: if her breath were as terrible as her terminations, there were no living near her, she would infect to the North Star. I would not marry her, though she were endowed with all that Adam had left him before he transgressed. She would have made Hercules have turned spit, yea, and have cleft his club to make the fire too. Come, talk not of her, you shall find her the infernal Ate in good apparel. I would to God some scholar would conjure her, for certainly, while she is here, a man may live as quiet in hell as in a sanctuary, and people sin upon purpose, because they would go thither; so indeed all disquiet, horror, and perturbation follows her.

Beatrice brings Claudio in his sulk to the Prince, as commanded, but not before she has caught most of what Benedick is saying against her. It takes the Prince to point out to Benedick that he can be heard. He leaves, but not without more insults, which Beatrice weathers. Before she is completely humiliated, she turns the tables and again tries to humiliate him in public. She refers to a possible earlier episode between them, where she gave him her heart only to be double-crossed – but she says she didn't want it anyway:

DON PEDRO Come, lady, come, you have lost the heart of
    Signior Benedick.
BEATRICE Indeed, my lord, he lent it me awhile, and I gave
    him use for it, a double heart for his single one. Marry,
    once before he won it of me with false dice, therefore your
    Grace may well say I have lost it.
DON PEDRO You have put him down, lady, you have put him
    down.
BEATRICE So I would not he should do me, my lord, lest I
    should prove the mother of fools.

In this instance she wins – any sort of liaison with Benedick would mean she might have idiots for children, or be the biggest idiot herself.

'We are the only love gods'

Don Pedro wants his friend Claudio to benefit from his wealth and power by helping him to marriage with Hero. He makes a public display of the betrothal and announces to all what has been going on. At this moment, when Claudio hears what his friend has done for him, he crosses the stage and hugs his benefactor, leaving Hero, his future wife, embarrassingly alone. Beatrice witnesses this, and we see what it is that she so readily scorns and that makes her protective of her cousin. This unhealthy split between the sexes is, of course, acceptable, but makes Beatrice angry inside, and it is this anger that fuels her. She becomes outspoken and lewd: 'Speak, cousin, or, if you cannot, stop his mouth with a kiss, and let not him speak neither'; and for the rest of the evening it is anger that drives her to drink harder than anyone else, dance faster than anyone else and laugh louder than anyone else. She's not alone: the Prince is also hell-bent on getting drunk. Beatrice plonks herself on his lap – the richest, most powerful person in the room – and flirts outrageously. Although there is a mutual connection between Beatrice and Don Pedro, they could never really understand what it's like to be each other. Beatrice could not know how lonely it is to be a prince; so even though they're enjoying themselves, there is an underlying sadness in the constant stream of jokes.

DON PEDRO Will you have me, lady?
BEATRICE No, my lord, unless I might have another for
    working days: your Grace is too costly to wear every day.
    But I beseech your Grace pardon me, I was born to speak
    all mirth and no matter.

And when the Prince says to Beatrice: 'Your silence most offends me, and to be merry best becomes you, for out o' question, you were born in a merry hour', to which she replies, 'No, sure, my lord, my mother cried . . .', how could he know her pain of not having a mother and how she has chosen to fight it and survive?

We improvised many times around the idea of Beatrice being adopted into Leonato's household as a young orphan, growing up as if she were Hero's sister but always knowing Leonato wasn't her father. Mrs Leonato is mentioned, but one imagines she died at some point (we never had a Mrs Leonato, only Aunt Ursula). That neither Beatrice nor Hero had a mother made the bond between them stronger, but Beatrice's own loss stayed private. I never settled on just one story for Beatrice's mother: I would imagine she died while giving birth – some terrible foul-up in the hands of an inept Victorian obstetrician; or I would imagine that her mother had never wanted a girl, and sobbed on hearing she'd had one, rejecting Beatrice even before the little baby had taken her first breath.

Beatrice is aware, however, that on some level she was given a gift: '. . . but then there was a star danced, and under that was I born.' Her mind is her gift, her saving grace. Her wonderful imagination became her salvation.

It is very true to life when Leonato says that Beatrice 'often dreamt of unhappiness and waked herself with laughing'. I remember a very difficult and unhappy time when I was growing up, when I woke myself up one morning laughing because the dream I was having was so funny, and I was very grateful to have been able to do that. It really helped. The things I imagined for Beatrice, or what we might have had in common, only became clear when I started rehearsing. You bring in what you can – even the smallest thing that might be relevant – and if necessary you multiply it by ten, or even a hundred, to make it useful. Improvising stories or scenarios around a theme in the play helps everyone to come together, building a collection of stories, no matter how fanciful, silly or offbeat. A collection of improvisations can help build the foundations of relationships. Sometimes you don't need to improvise. Matthew and I would talk about things that might have happened between Beatrice and Benedick. I would think of us sometimes as in that scene in *Terms of Endearment* when Shirley MacLaine and Jack Nicholson have had that disastrous date: it's all ruined and she asks him in for a coffee, and he says, 'I'd rather stick needles in my eyes.' You don't even have to share everything. I would imagine Benedick showing off in a green MG – I don't know why (they didn't even have green sports cars circa 1901), but it was one of those private images. Steve Mangan, who played Don Pedro, threw up in his party hat during one improvisation of the masked ball and I kept that image with me all through the run.

Amongst the rejoicing, the very drunk Prince decides to matchmake again and enlists the help of Leonato, Claudio and Hero, to 'undertake one of Hercules' labours, which is, to bring Signior Benedick and the Lady Beatrice into a mountain of affection th'one with th'other'. He's drunk, his best friend's getting married and he needs diversions. He can do whatever he wants: he is the Prince. 'For we are the only love-gods' is a declaration by a man about to use his power to manipulate people. Even though his purpose is to create enjoyment and do good, it feels dark nonetheless. His brother Don John is about to do the same – manipulate people – but for the purpose of causing pain and destruction. The play holds many such counterparts, has many mirror images: the good Prince and the dark Prince; two pairs of lovers, one the polar opposite to the other. It holds the light and the dark together, as if you can't have one without the other. In the humour there is sadness, and in the laughter there is anger.

'One man's meat is another man's poison' – Proverb

Don John's initial plans have been thwarted, but he is still looking for a way to 'cross this marriage'. In scene ii, Borachio says he believes he can devise a situation to convince Don Pedro and Claudio that Hero loves someone else. They will need proof of this – 'Proof enough to misuse the Prince, to vex Claudio, to undo Hero, and kill Leonato.'

Borachio is in favour with Margaret and he says he can persuade her to talk to him through Hero's window on the night before the wedding. Don Pedro and Claudio will then believe they have witnessed Hero talking to her lover. Don John agrees to 'put it in practice' and be 'constant in the accusation', offering Borachio a thousand ducats as a fee.

This cruel plan is mentioned at the end of the party and that small scene gave us the taste of what was to come. It was staged in a particular way: the music we had been listening and dancing to at the ball became disjointed, and the light darkened. Everyone moved slowly, and Don John was able to manipulate the other characters, quite literally. So, when each one was mentioned by name – whether it was Don Pedro, Claudio, Hero or Margaret – they were used as dummies almost, to show what was being planned. This strange, anarchic charade, heightened by the copious amounts of alcohol (I'd imagined) everyone had consumed, gave a chilling reality to the story.

'The world must be peopled'

In the garden the morning after (scene iii), Benedick has a talk with the audience, and we learn even more about his attitude to love and his friend behaving completely out of character. 'May I be so converted and see with these eyes? I cannot tell; I think not.' Benedick goes on to describe the perfect woman, 'but till all graces be in one woman, one woman shall not come in my grace', though he does make a concession to the colour of her hair: '– of what colour it please God!' This is his paradox: Benedick wants perfection but with such an attitude he stands a very good chance of never getting married to anyone. This seems to be a very modern problem. I've had conversations with friends who ask for dark eyes, or blond hair, a sense of humour and a car – all you have to do is look in the lonely hearts columns. All these requirements, when actually what it is really about is the relationship you have with yourself! But to see that, you have to leave yourself vulnerable, and this takes courage. Luckily for Benedick and Beatrice, they are given the opportunity to see themselves as others see them. The baiting scenes that happen next – first to Benedick and then to Beatrice – begin the process of transformation in each one.

In the garden Benedick overhears from the conversation between the Prince, Claudio and Leonato that Beatrice is in love with him. Knowing full well he can hear them, they go as far as they dare to 'Bait the hook well', and then even further, urging each other on as the conversation becomes more outrageous.

DON PEDRO Hath she made her affection known to
  Benedick?
LEONATO No, and swears she never will: that's her torment.
CLAUDIO 'Tis true indeed, so your daughter says: 'Shall I,' says
  she, 'that have so oft encountered him with scorn, write to
  him that I love him?'
LEONATO This says she now when she is beginning to write to
  him, for she'll be up twenty times a night, and there will
  she sit in her smock till she have writ a sheet of paper: my
  daughter tells us all.

CLAUDIO Now you talk of a sheet of paper, I remember a pretty jest your daughter told us of.

LEONATO O, when she had writ it, and was reading it over, she found 'Benedick' and 'Beatrice' between the sheet?

CLAUDIO That.

LEONATO O, she tore the letter into a thousand halfpence; railed at herself, that she should be so immodest to write to one that she knew would flout her. 'I measure him', says she, 'by my own spirit, for I should flout him, if he writ to me, yea, though I love him, I should.'

CLAUDIO Then down upon her knees she falls, weeps, sobs, beats her heart, tears her hair, prays, curses: 'O sweet Benedick! God give me patience!'

LEONATO She doth indeed, my daughter says so, and the ecstasy hath so much overborne her that my daughter is sometime afeard she will do a desperate outrage to herself: it is very true.

Benedick is then left alone, believing that he is loved – 'This can be no trick.' After he speaks the words 'Love me?', Benedick is caught out by the thought, and is unable to speak for a while, trying to control his emotions, because he's standing in front of a lot of people! He is beginning to show his vulnerability. 'Why, it must be requited' is his decision – his commitment; but he has a lot of back-pedalling to do, because his tormentors (and all those people in the audience) know him to 'have railed so long against marriage: but doth not the appetite alter?'

Benedick has thought himself unlovable and this, he reasoned, meant he could love no one in return. But somebody loves him: Beatrice loves him. Maybe it was Beatrice all along. He thought Beatrice could never love him, so he thought himself unlovable, so he loved no one. I imagine these characters wouldn't think inwardly in this analytical way. I would have these thoughts, but would remind myself that this was before Freud: these characters wouldn't have therapy. But 'somebody loves me' – like Shirley MacLaine (again) in *Sweet Charity*; when she sang that song, her heart opened with her voice. That's what I imagined. I used to stand in the wings and watch Benedick. I was about to come onstage to tell him about dinner and to sit in the garden and drink as much black coffee as I could (to chase away my imagined hangover). I would watch him and understand how lovable a character Benedick was, how brave and resilient and endearing, and honest. I would have to suppress these feelings and save them for later on because, to Beatrice, Benedick was still extremely annoying in the next short interchange. Not only would he not pick up on her jokes, but he seemed overly attentive, behaving disturbingly out of character, which made her think this might be his next line of attack, more cruel than his rudeness.

BEATRICE Against my will I am sent to bid you come in to dinner.
BENEDICK Fair Beatrice, I thank you for your pains.
BEATRICE I took no more pains for those thanks than you take pains to thank me; if it had been painful, I would not have come.
BENEDICK You take pleasure then in the message?
BEATRICE Yea, just so much as you may take upon a knife's point and choke a daw withal. You have no stomach, signior, fare you well.

Then it's Beatrice's turn. Under Don Pedro's instruction 'Let there be the same net spread for her', Hero and Ursula are going to fool Beatrice into thinking Benedick is in love with her.

Act III

'Speak low if you speak love'

Margaret is sent (by Hero) to coax Beatrice onstage, with the instruction,

> Whisper her ear, and tell her I and Ursley
> Walk in the orchard, and our whole discourse
> Is all of her . . .

Their plan works, 'For look where Beatrice like a lapwing runs / Close by the ground, to hear our conference,' and they begin to discuss Beatrice and talk of Benedick's 'love' for her. This is the most we ever hear Hero speak. I always imagined it was because Beatrice never allowed her any space to talk. Hero was also an extremely well-bred woman, therefore never said too much. I used to think this was another problem question: why doesn't she speak very much? If Shakespeare had wanted her to, he would have given her the words. For us, this was another example of having to 'do' the text, as a verb, as an action. Hero couldn't just not speak. She would at times go to speak then fail, or get interrupted, or not speak soon enough. Here she had the chance to talk and Beatrice was the one who had to shut up, or ruin her chance of overhearing what was said about her.

What Beatrice hears is earth-shattering. Hero says everything she has ever wanted to say about her cousin, enjoying the chance to get her own back and shake Beatrice off her pedestal, at the same time helping her to 'a good husband'. Of course, she would want what she thinks is best for Beatrice, while at the same time giving their friendship the chance to grow together – as wives as well as cousins; but as the Russian proverb we used in the programme says: 'Marriage sunders friends.'

Beatrice is a different sort of problem. She hears what she thinks is the truth, and listens, probably for the first time. She hears some awful things, and Shakespeare shows us the difference between Benedick and Beatrice in the way their friends talk about them in these scenes. It is a complete shock to her 'That Benedick loves Beatrice so entirely'; but the most telling moment is when she hears Hero say of her, 'She cannot love':

HERO
   ... But Nature never fram'd a woman's heart
   Of prouder stuff than that of Beatrice.
   Disdain and scorn ride sparkling in her eyes,
   Misprising what they look on, and her wit
   Values itself so highly that to her
   All matter else seems weak. She cannot love,
   Nor take no shape nor project of affection,
   She is so self-endeared.

To hear someone she knows so well say that she loves herself too much to be capable of loving; to realize that the outward show of pride and scorn and disdain has convinced others that she has no feelings, that

   her wit
   Values itself so highly that to her
   All matter else seems weak

– it is like a thunderbolt. She's been struck by lightning. She sees herself as others see her, and becomes vulnerable. And then to realize that somebody loves her, but that this person will be advised to 'fight against his passion' – that she may lose her chance with Benedick for ever – no wonder there is fire in her ears.

Beatrice is left alone to ask the audience for confirmation – '... Can this be true? / Stand I condemn'd for pride and scorn so much?' – and, of course, their silence is all she needs to confirm that it *is* true. Beatrice decides to change, but not without some struggle. She even develops a bad cold as a result.

She makes a determined effort to behave differently but thank God she heard all those brilliant things said about Benedick; she is still Beatrice after all, still vain. But to realize that she is not taken seriously, that she has paid a price for being the fool! She loves to make people laugh, but how lonely to be thought of as heartless. Beatrice has a heart, a big heart. You laughed at her attempt to reform, but I was moved by her courage to face herself.

'This looks not like a nuptial'

If it were not for Beatrice and Benedick you would think love did not exist in this play. In Act III, scene ii, the last scene before we took our interval, the play begins to turn and the darkness and violence take over. You could never describe *Much Ado About Nothing* as a gentle comedy, especially with a character like Don John, who 'will endeavour anything' (Act II, scene ii) to destroy the proceedings. The scene begins with Don Pedro and Claudio teasing the now lovesick Benedick, who is clutching a bunch of flowers. He has completely transformed himself, and Don Pedro and Claudio can't help themselves in making fun of him – their game is working so well. Benedick can bear it no longer and asks Leonato to 'walk aside', as he has something to discuss with him in private.

Don John finds Don Pedro and Claudio alone, and does exactly what he says he will: sets the wheels in motion to ruin and shatter everyone's lives. He tells them:

DON JOHN . . . the lady is disloyal.
CLAUDIO Who, Hero?
DON JOHN Even she – Leonato's Hero, your Hero, every man's Hero.
CLAUDIO Disloyal?
DON JOHN The word is too good to paint out her wickedness. I could say she were worse; think you of a worse title and I will fit her to it . . .

What he says is brutal, misogynistic and vicious. He goes further. For proof he tells them 'go but with me tonight, you shall see her chamber-window entered, even the night before her wedding-day'. We already know that this is going to happen and how; and before our eyes it does. In all the theatres we played, Hero would appear, then Margaret would take her place and Borachio was seen to scale the wall to reach her.

A sort of dumb show, or silent movie, was made out of what was being said. I don't know if Shakespeare would have physicalized the language in quite the same way as we did, but I believe he meant it to be that obvious. Nowadays it is so much harder to visualize the spoken word, we are so reliant on television and film to paint the pictures for us. I believe Shakespeare intended his language to be like pictures – as if you could see the images as the characters spoke them. His language is immediate and, when brought to life, is exciting to hear. There are many ways to do it, but I loved this oppprtunity for choice; and this information was the catalyst necessary to drive the play deeper into despair.

The second half of our production of the play began with Act III, scene iii, the night before the wedding.

Even though we can sense disaster drawing near, new characters are introduced: Dogberry and Verges, two of Shakespeare's clowns. Shakespeare's company of actors at the time of *Much Ado About Nothing* was called 'The Lord Chamberlain's Men', and the popular clown of the company was Will Kempe. His name, rather than 'Dogberry', appeared in the Quarto edition (1600) of *Much Ado About Nothing*, evidence that Shakespeare wrote the part specifically for this comic actor, as he did that of Verges for Richard Cowley, the pale and skinny straight man.

The story so far has centred on a socially exclusive wealthy elite – the highbrow – but now Shakespeare focuses on the underbelly of society, the lowbrow. Dogberry and Verges make us laugh with their ineptitude, but they uncover the truth. The clowns bring clarity, and this is the ultimate paradox – as with Oedipus, who lost his sight when he understood and saw the truth, so the confused unravel the confusion. Dogberry doesn't even speak good English. He jumbles up his words and has a sort of verbal dyslexia. Yet he is the one who speaks sense. Dogberry and Verges are giving instructions to the nightwatchmen, telling them to pay specific attention to 'Signior Leonato's door, for the wedding being there tomorrow, there is a great coil tonight'.

No sooner are the nightwatchmen left alone in the dark than Borachio and Conrade enter and Borachio is overheard telling Conrade that he has earned a large sum of money from Don John because they have managed to deceive Don Pedro and Claudio into thinking Hero is unfaithful. So Don John's plan has worked. The nightwatchmen arrest Borachio and

Conrade and take them away (in our production the constables were complete with helmets, truncheons and handcuffs).

'Love and a cough cannot be hid' – Proverb

On the morning of the wedding (scene iv) Margaret is helping Hero dress, and they talk of fashion and sex; when Beatrice arrives she gets teased mercilessly about Benedick. I never solved Beatrice having a cold – except that to be in love is to be unwell, as Benedick says in Act III, scene i. The Chinese believe a cold is a sign of change.

Leonato is also preparing himself for the wedding (scene v), but he gets interrupted by Dogberry and Verges to say they have arrested two men 'and we would have them this morning examined before your worship'. Leonato tells them to do it themselves; he has no time for these two, as the wedding party is waiting. Leonato leaves for the church, little knowing what he has just missed.

Act IV

'My griefs cry louder than advertisement'

The guests are waiting in the church and a chorus of 'Jesu Joy' was sung, with the men and the women taking separate harmonies. The stage was clear and so we entered down an imaginary aisle and took our places in imaginary pews, the bride's family on the left, the groom's party on the right. Just as the Friar is about to join them together, 'You come hither, my lord, to marry this lady?', Claudio simply answers, 'No'.

Shakespeare comes straight to the point in this scene: we're only on line five and the whole proceeding stops for a moment with this shocking rejection. Leonato attempts to lighten the misunderstanding, but Claudio means what he says and quite literally takes Hero by the hand and calmly walks her over to her father: 'There, Leonato, take her back again. / Give not this rotten orange to your friend . . .' And Claudio continues, as he calls on everyone, both onstage and in the auditorium, to share his outrage, his hurt and his humiliation. He describes her in the most awful ways: 'She knows the heat of a luxurious bed: / Her blush is guiltiness, not modesty'; he says he means '. . . not to knit [his] soul / To an approved wanton'; and to Hero herself:

> But you are more intemperate in your blood
> Than Venus, or those pamper'd animals
> That rage in savage sensuality.

– he believes himself to be so utterly in the right, that he is the injured party.

Claudio included the audience when he said:

Would you not swear,
All you that see her, that she were a maid,
By these exterior shows?

and he brought up the houselights. We onstage were caught as much as the audience, all of us being asked to judge her. The theatre became one huge, awful courtroom, and Claudio got down off the stage as he continued to shame her, walking amongst the audience, forcing Leonato, then Hero, to talk to him across the heads of the audience. We all became her jury.

Beatrice is watching all this with horror, witnessing the downfall of an innocent woman, helpless to do anything about it. The Prince shocks everyone when he says, 'I stand dishonour'd, that have gone about / To link my dear friend to a common stale [whore].' We changed the word 'stale' to 'whore' – the intended meaning. Stale is not a word alive to us today; it doesn't have the power the word 'whore' does, and it is one of the intentions of the word: to shock.

The Prince and Don John support Claudio's accusations and, finally, so does Leonato when he says, 'Hath no man's dagger here a point for me?' Leonato is a broken man, at which point Hero faints, unable to believe what is happening, betrayed by her own father. Don Pedro, Don John and Claudio leave the church.

Everyone is in a panic thinking Hero might die under the weight of such injustice. Leonato wants her to die: 'Do not live, Hero, do not ope thine eyes . . .' He wants to kill her for what he believes she has done and he totally disowns her. She used to be his, and his alone, his property –

But mine, and mine I lov'd, and mine I prais'd,
And mine that I was proud on – mine so much

>   That I myself was to myself not mine,
>   Valuing of her ...

– but now she is dirty and he can't bear it. He was the proud father, in love with his daughter, and now she has brought disgrace upon his household. He disapproved of her cousin: she was too outspoken. He wanted nothing more but for Hero to marry well. Both he and Claudio are guilty of objectifying Hero and they suffer because of it. They think of her as a 'jewel', their 'rich and precious gift', 'Dian in her orb / As chaste as is the bud ere it be blown', 'the sweetest lady' – and this is part of the sexist vocabulary that is in the play and that highlights the great divide between the sexes that Beatrice has been trying to escape from.

The Friar tries to calm the furious Leonato, for he believes, as Beatrice does, that Hero is innocent. The Friar suggests they claim she has, in fact, died. This news may soften Claudio's heart. If not, it would be better to

>   ... conceal her,
>   As best befits her wounded reputation.
>   In some reclusive and religious life ...

– in other words: put her in a convent. Benedick supports the Friar's plan, encouraging Leonato to go along with it. Benedick and Beatrice are then left alone together.

Beatrix: 'she who blesses'

BENEDICK Lady Beatrice, have you wept all this while?
BEATRICE Yea, and I will weep a while longer.
BENEDICK I will not desire that.
BEATRICE You have no reason, I do it freely.
BENEDICK Surely I do believe your fair cousin is wronged.

The next dialogue between them, shows how powerfully these two love. The humour of having seen them fall off their respective high horses is turned into one of the most emotionally true scenes of the play. They both show themselves to be loyal, courageous and passionate. Benedick tries to comfort her, as they try to deal with what has just happened. Even though they are talking of serious things, they can't help themselves in joking with each other. It happens despite their feelings: they bring out the humour in each other, and now that we see them together as possible lovers, this witty repartee feels like intimacy.

However, Beatrice is her contrary self, and can't commit – is frightened to say what her heart feels, especially after witnessing such an awful wedding. She keeps stopping herself,

BEATRICE . . . It were as possible for me to say I loved nothing so well as you, but believe me not; and yet I lie not; I confess nothing, nor I deny nothing. I am sorry for my cousin.

She tries to reason that it is because she is so upset that she keeps changing what she is saying. Benedick believes Hero is innocent and Beatrice wants revenge, and when finally Benedick walks into her thoughts by asking, 'Come, bid me do anything for thee', Beatrice asks him to kill his best friend. It's not until Benedick finally declines that Beatrice's fury is unleashed. Not only is she enraged by what these other men have done to her cousin, but Benedick will not see what a villain Claudio is. So she tries to throw aside the love she was about to confess, feelings that were so difficult for her to admit to, but that were there ('I love you with so much of my heart that none is left to protest').

I believe if Benedick hadn't eventually conceded to her demand, she would never have spoken to him again – that her hatred of him would now be true. All the times she has put

Benedick down, all the slanders and insults, were almost a way of keeping him in her consciousness. By allowing feelings of love to grow for him, she must have realized how deep they went; and her scorn and frustration in these next speeches are coloured by her anger at Benedick. 'Kill Claudio' is not only a terrible thing to ask of him, but it is what's in her heart – a deadly thought, exposing her, and he rejects her. 'There is no love in you,' she says, and the truth of that realization hits her hard, causing her even more pain. She hits out with her words – so much so that Benedick finds it impossible to interrupt. She pulls all men down, wishing again and again that she were one, crying out against this sexual inequality: 'O, that I were a man for his sake, or that I had any friend would be a man for my sake!' – she feels impotent as a woman, and yet more of a man than the men – 'But manhood is melted into curtsies . . .'

Benedick finally manages to calm her down – 'Think you in your soul the Count Claudio hath wronged Hero?' – which makes her stop and listen to him, hoping her assurance will satisfy him: 'Yea, as sure as I have a thought, or a soul.' Convinced, Benedick agrees to challenge Claudio, and with his declaration he takes over, becoming chivalrous, strong and, in Beatrice's estimation, different from other men. This is the point at which she allows herself to fall deeply, madly in love with him, which she probably was all along.

Benedick and Beatrice are misfits, but they have, thankfully, found each other. They have warmth and wit; they represent hope and love and give the play its heart. It was important to feel that these two could love in this otherwise harsh and cynical world.

'When the age is in, the wit is out'

In scene ii the Sexton (with a little help from Dogberry and Verges) interrogates Borachio and Conrade, and the Nightwatchmen tell what they overheard. The Sexton informs them all: 'Prince John is this morning secretly stolen away [I found it most telling that he escaped – the coward]: Hero was in this manner accused, in this very manner refused, and upon the grief of this suddenly died.'

In conclusion, the prisoners are to be brought to Leonato so that he may know the truth. The prisoners' frustration and Dogberry's malapropisms and confused language lead Conrade to insult him to his face as he is led to Leonato's: 'Away! You are an ass, you are an ass.' Dogberry talks to the audience and asks them to help him remember that Conrade insulted him: 'But masters, remember that I am an ass: though it be not written down, yet forget not that I am an ass.' He makes direct contact, showing us a part of himself – letting us see his vulnerability – and so we have the chance to look behind our attitude and think of him as not just an ass but as a 'fellow that hath had losses'; we are given the chance to see this man as someone with real emotions.

Act V

'Boys, apes, braggarts, Jacks, milksops!'

The play has become more abstract, moving along at a faster pace. Declan reflected this in the staging, doing away with entrances and exits, dovetailing scenes and keeping the actors onstage throughout the final act, which gave the play a fluidity. The actors not involved in the scenes would form a sort of chorus, creating a shape around those speaking, almost as if eavesdropping. All the cast were onstage through to the end, bringing focus and unity to the story.

Antonio [Ursula] is trying to get Leonato to pull himself together, but Leonato will not be counselled. He is grieving – 'My soul doth tell me Hero is belied' – crying into his brandy (one of the few props in the second half was Leonato's brandy glass). They are interrupted by the Prince and Claudio. Leonato channels his grief and challenges Claudio, presenting him with his glove:

> Thou hast so wrong'd mine innocent child and me,
> That I am forc'd to lay my reverence by,
> And with grey hairs and bruise of many days
> Do challenge thee to trial of a man.

In our production, when the Prince and Claudio would not take him seriously, Ursula [Antonio] took over. She berated them, and had to be dragged away; she could not contain her rage. It was very unexpected to see this older woman courageously attempting to tell these men off. She grabbed that glove and hit Claudio with it.

Benedick finds Don Pedro and Claudio and takes Claudio aside to challenge him. Whereas before he came on with a bunch of flowers behind his back, Benedick now holds the symbolic white glove. They try to tease and mock Benedick as before – almost a mirror of the baiting scene; but Benedick has changed: he is growing up, and Claudio and Don Pedro now seem like spoiled children, or worse, immature adolescents, in the face of Benedick's genuine strength. He calls Claudio 'boy' and 'Lord Lackbeard', and tells Don Pedro, 'I must discontinue your company'; and the last piece of sobering news is: 'Your brother the bastard is fled from Messina.' Benedick is serious for the first time.

Dogberry passes by with Borachio and Conrade, and Don Pedro asks him why his brother's men have been arrested. Borachio confesses all to the Prince. Leonato arrives (with Antonio [Ursula] and the Sexton) to question Borachio. Now that everyone is beginning to understand what has happened, Don Pedro and Claudio beg Leonato's forgiveness. Leonato insists they 'Possess the people in Messina here / How innocent she died', and that Claudio must marry his niece, 'Almost the copy of my child that's dead'. Claudio agrees. Borachio defends Margaret's part in the deception, saying she

> knew not what she did when she spoke to me,
> But always hath been just and virtuous
> In anything that I do know by her.

'They would talk themselves mad'

In scene ii Benedick asks Margaret to fetch Beatrice. He tells the audience he is trying to woo her by writing her a love poem, but he's not doing very well. (The 'chorus' moved to stand as close to Benedick as they could, in order to read over his shoulder the rhyme he was reading out; but eventually he gave up: 'I was not born under a rhyming planet, nor I cannot woo in festival terms.'

Beatrice appears – I stepped out from the chorus – but again they play with words so much together that they can't get through to the courtship. Benedick tries to kiss Beatrice right at the beginning, but she successfully avoids it by talking rather than kissing. In amongst the joking and the passion is the terrible deed that Benedick has promised to undertake. She needs proof that Benedick is carrying out his promise, and there shall be no kissing until Beatrice has discovered from Benedick 'what hath passed between [him] and Claudio'. Benedick persists, and almost gives up – 'Thou and I are too wise to woo peaceably' – before he moves in on her again, almost cornering her with his wit, and attempts to kiss her one more time. This time she can't move; he gets closer and closer – 'Serve God, love me, and mend' – but just then they are interrupted by Ursula the servant's voice, and unfortunately for Beatrice she never gets that kiss.

In the brief scene (iii) at Leonato's monument, Claudio does what he promised Leonato and hangs an epitaph at Hero's tomb for everyone to see; and during his act of remorse the dark night ends and dawn breaks.

The final scene is the day of the reconciliatory wedding. Before Claudio arrives for the ceremony, Benedick asks for the Friar's help, when the time comes, in marrying him to Beatrice. The Prince and Claudio arrive as promised and then the ladies enter in masks. Claudio, once immature and spoiled by the attention of the Prince, has by now developed a sense of humility. Addressing his bride-to-be, he offers: 'I am your husband if you like of me'; and Hero's 'cousin' is revealed to be Hero herself.

At the tomb, we saw a more emotional Claudio; he showed

his feelings for the first time, and his fall from grace, and this public display of weakness gave me the idea that he was capable now more than before of being a loving and wise husband to Hero.

'Here dwells Benedick, the married man'

Benedick takes his chance and calls out from the auditorium, 'Which is Beatrice?' The houselights are brought up and there is an echo of that other morning, a healing of that tragic day. Beatrice hears her name spoken by the one who loves her and she is put on the spot but still cannot admit in public how she feels. He asks, 'Then you do not love me?' and she replies, 'No, truly, but in friendly recompense.'

The others intervene by producing two bizarre pieces of paper, one 'Fashion'd to Beatrice' from Benedick, swearing he loves her, and the other from Beatrice, 'Containing her affection unto Benedick'. (Beatrice felt so scared that this might be read out in front of Benedick and everyone else that she managed to grab the paper from her cousin's hand and eat it – not in Shakespeare's script!) This is reminiscent of the make-believe letter that you hear Leonato and Claudio allude to in Benedick's baiting scene:

LEONATO O, she tore the letter into a thousand halfpence;
    railed at herself, that she should be so immodest to write
    to one that she knew would flout her. 'I measure him', says
    she, 'by my own spirit, for I should flout him, if he writ to
    me, yea, though I love him, I should.'

    (Act II, scene iii)

One of Benedick's most endearing qualities is his constant humour: 'Come, I will have thee, but by this light I take thee for pity', to which she replies, 'I would not deny you, but by this good day I yield upon great persuasion, and partly to save your life, for I was told you were in a consumption.' This is the last remark she makes, because Benedick does at last kiss her.

We held that kiss for a very long time. It used to remind me of Rhett Butler in *Gone With The Wind*, when he says to Scarlet, 'You need kissing, badly. That's what's wrong with you. You should be kissed and often, and by someone who knows how.' To kiss for the first time is the most crucial point in any love story. Emil Ludwig said, 'It changes the relationship of two people much more strongly than even the final surrender, because this kiss already has within it that surrender.' I loved it because I knew what was in that kiss: I was kissing the one I'd fought so hard not to love. In this world, where words are easily misconstrued, kisses are eloquent. What could Beatrice say after that? He took her breath away.

As everything is resolving itself, Claudio says to Benedick what to me seems an odd thing, but true to character,

> I had well hoped thou wouldst have denied Beatrice, that I might have cudgelled thee out of thy single life, to make thee a double-dealer; which out of question thou wilt be, if my cousin do not look exceeding narrowly to thee.

At this point in our production, another choice was made to clarify the text, although it was not a conventional or standard choice: Claudio held out his hand to Beatrice, in reconciliation. Beatrice, unable to entirely forgive him, stepped away, rejecting his offer of friendship. It took Benedick to say, 'Come, come, we are friends,' to encourage her to shake his hand. It was one of the many details that added colour and subtext to the play. It was unexpected but believable: I knew Claudio would be a good husband to Hero, but I wasn't so sure how long it would be before he reverted to type. On the other hand, I imagined that Benedick and Beatrice were in for an interesting, inspiring and fulfilled marriage, full of humour and love but not without the odd disagreement.

The news that Don John has been 'ta'en in flight / And brought with armed men back to Messina' is a sort of closure – the cycle is complete. As our Don John was brought up onstage from the auditorium, it was a reflection of his arrival in Act I, scene I; but not even Don John's return can dampen everyone's spirits. Benedick calls for the pipers to play and the celebrations to begin with dancing: 'Strike up, pipers!'

Conclusion

> For there is nothing sillier than a silly laugh.
>
> Catullus (*c.*84–*c.*54 BC)

'I humbly give you leave to depart'

We interpreted *Much Ado About Nothing* in our own way, making what might be considered unconventional choices, and surprising our audiences; but the play, for all I have said about the darkness we discovered in it, is very funny. Declan has a genius for bringing out the comedy in Shakespeare. He encouraged us to take things to their limit, or to their natural conclusion – like Beatrice eating the paper: if you consider all that has been said up to that point, and then make an imaginative leap, it makes absolute sense that she would react in this way. It confirmed what I knew about her and how I wanted her to be thought of: she would rather die than let her love of Benedick be publicly known. She doesn't want to risk being humiliated in front of people. She's proud, and quick, and anarchic. The audience get an idea of Benedick's attempt at a love letter, but they never know what Beatrice wrote, because she ate her words. It wasn't a very large piece of paper, so I could get it in my mouth quite quickly – but obviously – and it made the audience laugh.

There was a lot of laughter, on the stage and in the auditorium, and it was important to hear the characters laughing. Laughter was a valuable detail, as there were many different ways to laugh and it brought the text to life. It also showed Benedick and Beatrice as successful entertainers. You could laugh *at* someone, laugh because someone had said something funny, laugh to hide embarrassment, laugh instead of crying, laugh to be polite, try not to laugh, and laugh at your own jokes – Benedick's speciality.

I really found something out when we worked on the voices of these characters. Joan Washington, a very experienced and unique voice coach was invited to join us at rehearsal. She talked to us about upper-class accents in comparison to our own, and how the different use of vowels could express a kind of confidence. I discovered that by elongating my vowels, accentuating the poshness, I gave the impression of being incredibly self-assured. It had the effect of flattening out the sentences, which in turn helped the comedy of the language; and I didn't just elongate them a bit, but a lot. Quite a number of Declan's notes to me after performances were about keeping the vowels long. This was the hardest part. I felt I was running a huge risk, taking my time to speak in this way, and I couldn't imagine getting away with it; but I remember reading a quote of Prunella Scales (which also illustrates how actors feed off one another) saying that to get the best humour from a sentence you should be economical with the emphasis: one word at the most should be emphasized:

I think it's more a question of phrasing. Phrasing and stress. I learned about this through John Gielgud. Janet Suzman told me once that when she was going to play Saint Joan, Gielgud said to her, 'Don't forget that in Shaw, there's only one main stress in every sentence.' And I've found that true not only of Shaw but of almost everything: of colloquial speech, of mannered speech in Restoration comedy, of situation comedy on television. Rationing the stresses like this isn't dull, it's the reverse of dull: it makes

speech rapid, shifting and varied and is very good for
comedy.*

The voices we were finding pulled the aristocratic characters together as a group, especially when accompanied by the
work on the graceful movements and the posturing of this
ruling class. I also realized that an accent took the pressure
away from having to entertain, and I stopped indicating that
she was funny, as with a red nose, or a punchline – another
paradox: acting seems to be made up of paradoxes. Or is that
just like life?

We rehearsed the way the characters would move with Jane
Gibson. She taught us the manners and etiquette and posture
(the corsets would help too – I wore mine in rehearsals pretty
much from the beginning); she would have us walk about the
room in our groups, the men and the women. I would do cir-
cuits, with my back straight and a book on my head – sort of
'Beatrice at finishing school'. The dances for the masked ball
were all about men on one side and women on the other; and
this division was further emphasized in the songs that Paddy
Cuneen taught us, as the harmonies required the women to
sing one part and the men another. (The garden tea-party we
improvised – which later became most of the first act – found
the men grouping together and being served tea and sandwiches by some of the women.) This formality in the body
and voice was an enormous help in achieving an impression
of the high status and social rank to which Beatrice belonged,
even though she was on the outside.

Nick had the men in uniforms of bottle green and cream,
in the Edwardian style right down to the constables' helmets.
The men wore high-waisted trousers and facial hair. Steve

* Quoted from Peter Barkworth, *About Acting*, Methuen, p. 49

Mangan grew a moustache and Matthew stuck his on. The women were in long petticoats and skirts; Beatrice wore a shirt and tie at the beginning and a huge hat for the sun. There were parasols, with Hero's in a prettier lace. As the story went on, the jackets were off in the garden with the sleeves rolled up, morning coffee and cigars; and after the terrible wedding, black was worn for the mourning of Hero's 'death', which added to the darkness that descended – the stage was white, with long white banners creating columns to give height and space and a backdrop for Judith Greenwood's lighting. So we could have tall trees, or cathedral pillars, with entrances around and behind them. It looked simple and beautiful.

I haven't really talked about the use of verse and prose in *Much Ado About Nothing*; that's because Beatrice doesn't speak a lot of verse – I think her only bit of iambic pentameter is at the end of Act III, scene i: 'What fire is in mine ears . . .' Hero speaks mainly in verse, and this soliloquy is at the end of Hero's scene. Verse is prominent in more tragic moments, but the comedy is invariably in prose. You could write a whole other book on prose versus poetry, but it was not something we discussed objectively in rehearsal. It is something that works on the actor and audience as it happens. You may not know the characters are speaking in verse, but you can feel the difference. It is actual, physical and real. Use it how you will, I suppose.

I find verse harder to speak. I used to find it very hard, until I made myself remember which words ended the lines of verse. John Barton once pulled me up on this – 'Do you know the words at the end of the lines?' Well, I do now; I can't imagine learning my lines without taking such note. It also has its own meaning if you take the line endings out of context and do this with the words that fall on the first beat, too. It's just a game really, because when you perform, you have to sort of forget about all this – play the game of forgetting in order to create space and clear the mind.

Overall, the work we did was divided, in Declan's words, between the visible and the invisible. Rehearsals and research, practice and improvising are the invisible work, and the performance, well, is the visible; but the characters themselves can be divided in this way, and what is interesting is when the audience get a chance to see the invisible in characters. Watching Beatrice and Don Pedro drink too much is seeing some sort of subtext being played out, or when Beatrice won't let go of Benedick's hand when he agrees to challenge Claudio at the end of Act IV, scene i.

Declan didn't just regurgitate Shakespeare; he found a way to make it workable and managed to appeal to different audiences by exploring what interested him in the play; and in so doing he kept the story fresh and alive and relevant, without being self-conscious.

I am still baffled that Shakespeare's words can cause a reaction in an audience even after four hundred years. How is it possible that he understood the human heart so well? We don't seen to be that different to the people he wrote for.